Rainbows and Rainy Days

Q. M. Saiyed

BookLeaf Publishing

Presentation by *BookLeaf Publishing*

Web: www.bookleafpub.com

E-mail: info@bookleafpub.com

ISBN: 9789357446822

First edition 2022

Table of Contents

Favourite Colour

How can I choose a colour for my own,
When there's a world of diverse shades?
How can I select a favourite from the rainbow,
When it lifts me up on a difficult day?

I've spent the darkest nights,
Pleading with a near black sky,
But by mid afternoon, it's the brightest blue,
Filling me with hope, with its streaks of golden
hues.

I've sat under the shade of a great willow tree,
Its beautifully sad leaves lamenting in the
breeze,
Their shade of green, sparkling with silver tears
From the mighty and majestic clouds above.

I have marvelled in the presence of the
marvellous moon
And its cleverly-reflecting, white glow.
I've watched the glorious stars wink one by one,
Displaying their own spectacular show.

I've smiled at a rainbow of flowers as they salsa
in the sun
And dipped my toes in the splendid sea,
A silent, sublime, iridescent treat,
Lapping on the silky, smooth, honey shore.

The white peaks of the magnificent mountain,
The textured peels of a hundred fruits,
The enchantment of a thousand sunsets
Fills me with life anew.

The fiery power and beauty of the tiger
Are like the words of a William Blake poem.
A floating feather in the whistling wind
Lures me in, taking me to places where I'm
much lighter.

The spectacular flash as a robin passes,
The bright splash of the blood in my vessels,
The myogenic, pumping home of love in my
chest,
In which people have left their gashes.

The deepest brown of my doe eyes blinking and
The soft caramel curves of my skin,
The ebony of my inherited curls
Stand as reminders of my ancestral lands.

How can I choose a colour for my own

When there's a world of diverse shades?
How can I select a favourite from the rainbow,
When it lifts me up on a difficult day?

A Narcissist's Confession

I read your emotions like the words in a book.
My fingers trace the details of your cover.
I predict your chapter endings and influence
your story,
To my liking, because you belong to me, a mere
possession.
Ascend with me to the skies and then fall from
glory,
Like a rose in full bloom, crushed in my palm.
Then I'll drag you to hell: the storm before the
calm.

Lady in Red

My steady streams of garnet flow
Like abundant rivers of tears.
Piercing stares from your stealthy eyes
Hit like the sharpest arrows on my breasts.
I'm a blood diamond.

My existence glistens like rubies
Against the dullness of the earth.
You say what you want, do as you please,
No consequences for a supreme sex.
I'm a blood diamond.

My crimson shield protects me still,
From the countless fingers pointing blame,
Easy target, wilting from the weight,
Like a poppy in a gust of wind.
I'm a blood diamond.

You cut off the auburn fires of my hair
Like your red flags destroy my womb.
Your hand's larger than mine and it chokes
My flesh until I'm left with bones.
I'm a blood diamond.

I hide scarlet truths like gems in a mine,
In the Divine gift keeping me alive.
My electric emotions form currents,
That you influence to suit your lies.
I'm a blood diamond.

You open me up like a treasure chest,
Stealing like a colonising thief,
A trapped rose in a cage, withering,
Spoilt by your manipulating tricks.
I'm a blood diamond.

A skin as thick as the bark of an oak
In autumn with its mahogany leaves,
I steer gracefully through time's troubles,
Like a vine in a forest of death.
I'm a blood diamond.

What is Grief?

Can I tell you what grief is?
It's the absence of air in your breath.
It's the life in the word that is 'death'.

Can I tell you what grief is?
It's the sound of a shattering mind,
It's past, present and future entwined.

Can I tell you what grief is?
It's the spinning Earth when the world stops;
It's burning heat when temperatures drop.

Can I tell you what grief is?
It's loneliness in a lively room;
It's the feeling of impending doom.

Can I tell you what grief is?
It's the guilt, shame, regret and longing,
Until, in grief, you find belonging.

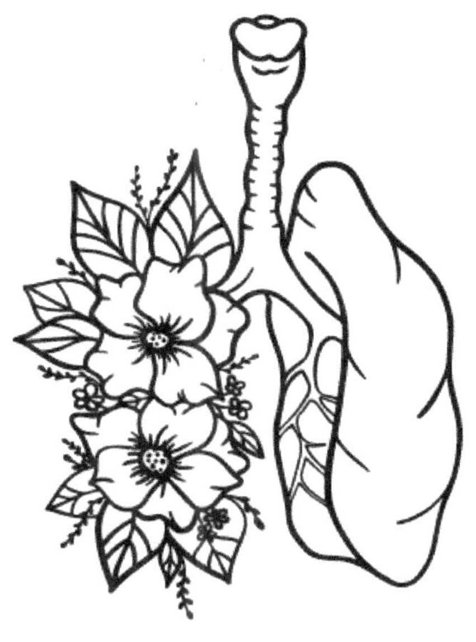

Betrayed

I wear this badge with my head held high,
A branding, a reminder of a past life.
Thrusting their knives, they disguised as allies,
Like a murderer acting as a midwife.

I walked into a battlefield unarmed;
Their arrows came raining down like confetti.
I disguised my pain, like I was unharmed,
As they laughed and slashed me with machetes.

My legs collapsed beneath the weight of my
bones;
I lay withering and bleeding to death,
Crying amongst the silent tombstones,
Betrayed, I breathed my penultimate breaths.

But something descended from the Heavens
above,
Invisible to the enemies.
A power that goes by the name of Love,
To alleviate all the agonies.

Enveloping me in a warm embrace,
Bringing kindness and hope to a frozen world.
Beautifully painting over the disgrace,
A second life into existence swirled.

Just a Haircut?

Silky strands drop,
Make your angry silence stop.
Hold your breath...
I'm going for the chop.
Memories of you fall one by one.
I guess this means we're really done.
Trying my best not to peer down at you,
Or the burdens that weighed a tonne.
Your menace in my locks,
Gives hidden, calculated shocks.
I say a soundless prayer,
And in this healing, get lost.
The slow and steady snipping,
The beat of my heart skipping,
Means this can't be just a haircut,
As I feel your fingers gripping.
The blackness tumbles down my back.
I brace myself for the attack,
But that's it; you're going...
I'm regaining what I once lacked.

A Song and Dance

There's a blanket of scars beneath her layers of
skin.
There are anxieties that are carried deep within.
No one knows tomorrow; she doesn't worry
about today.
The veiling night is still young, and there's time
for a cabaret.

She lets her fragile heart spread its wings under
a thousand lights,
Taking her delicate mind of glass to brave new
heights.
Her blushing cheeks tell the story of her timidity,
While several eyes and hands seek her
availability.

She carries herself with class, despite the hours
of the dark,
And voices her truths in pleasant melodies like a
lark.
Her rouged lips display a deceiving confidence,
And her scant, seductive, flamingo outfit
misrepresents

the reality of her haunted, tempest-swept soul,
Which burns in the core of her being, like a
furnace of coal.
Her Tango, Quickstep and Rumba are a flying
escape,
Concealing her secrets like an elaborate drape.

She wines, dazzles and drops in magenta,
Absorbing happiness like nutrients from a
placenta,
But soon, the positivity and song of the night
will die,
And she'll be forced to lamentably wave to her
mind, goodbye.

Friends From Space

A beacon of light,
A glimmer of hope,
Appeasing our plights
With some ways to cope.

Floating together,
Through a field of stars,
As light as feathers,
Remedying scars.

Rotating like Earth,
A sensual dance,
A trying rebirth,
Deeper than romance.

Our planets collide,
When life throws its spears,
Our fate coincides,
And strength reappears.

With moons being in sync,
Somehow we just know,
A sky full of ink
Will set us aglow.

Phoenix Rising

You hid me in a wooden chest,
Locked it, then threw away the key.
I fought and failed, so distressed,
A gullible detainee.

My tears stung and skin was aflame,
As my diminished self-love spoke,
Burning guilt and endless shame,
With betrayal, you revoke.

Soon enough, the chest was ablaze,
With me, the fuel of the fire.
Now ashes sprouting bouquets,
The chest served to be my pyre.

But a yellow-orange-red lamp,
Miniscule at first, then grew,
Like the hearth of a great camp,
Which was suddenly imbued.

The will to fight suddenly rung,
My heart began to beat again,
Body from the ashes sprung,
Lights filling the room, and then…

Rugged wings birthed from shoulder blades,
Leathery, thick skin smoothed over,
Now you'll lose every crusade;
I found my four-leafed clover.

I wear my feathers like a crown,
Bejewelled, earning every glint,
I soar above your dead town
And your lifeless heart of flint.

Never look at me with those eyes;
I have found myself, distinguished;
You learnt a phoenix's cries
Can never be extinguished.

Guarded

I cement bricks together,
Build a wall as high as a night out,
A tower, like Rapunzel's.
But I'm no prisoner here,
Or am I?
These secretive grey stones shout.
My fate is crystal clear.
It's glittered in the sky:
It's me, myself and I.

Holiday

Perfectly blended sunsets
And early, luminous dawns,
A scene from a romcom film
And lazy afternoon yawns,

Scenery picture perfect,
Troubles temporarily,
Dissipate into warm air,
Forgotten so merrily,

A plethora of good times,
Making memories to last,
Sand in toes whilst reading,
The azure sea so clear, vast,

Roaming streets, riding taxis,
Laughing to the gut's content,
More new experiences,
Existing facts it augments,

Well-rounded and tolerant,
Cultured and open-minded,
Thinking outside the dull box,
A holiday's due, admitted.

Utopia to Dystopia

Our planet is a pearl, protected and free;
Sometimes it embodies a beautiful banshee.
She supplies springs of hope and waterfalls
deep,
Or are these merely the tears she's forced to
weep?

Our planet provides bounties in abundance,
For those who refuse to practise coexistence.
She births vegetation and mountains so high,
Yet Nature's starving and poverty is rife.

Our planet brings day and the precious gift of
night;
Instead of beauty sleep, crimes are pledged, out
of sight.
She carefully carves and crafts mines of
cherished gems,
But humans cultivate thorns on her flowers'
stems.

Our planet is green, brown and a brilliant blue;
White caps are melting but corporations tell
others what to do.

She gave a utopia, perfectly intact,
We made it a dystopia, a planet racked.

Troublesome You

You're the water that quenches a thirst;
I guzzle you down, greedy for more.
You're the race in which I win first,
And then set off on a world tour.
You're promises kept and happy tears wept,
And a rescue dinghy that reaches the shore.

You're a fleece snuggie on a rainy day;
I embrace you and squeeze you tight.
You're the shoulders to lean on and stay,
And the voice that makes my soul take flight.
You're a million reasons and rhymes to live,
Even when you're high as a kite.

You're the final piece in my puzzle,
A funny childhood memory shared.
You have all the innocence of Abel
And the complexity of Caine bared.
Your words cushion my falls like cotton wool,
With the power to see a wronged soul repaired.

You're an electric blue that excites my being,
The youth of yellow, exaggerated.
There's a lulling in your teal that's freeing,

Baby pink vulnerability. Understated.
You're a multicoloured pleasure, a rainbow,
Worth more than the treasures of the world,
amalgamated.

Yemen

'So random! Is that even a country?' she asked.

Yes. The poorest in the Middle East with a heart
        the size of the continent.

Yes. It's where my Prophet set his blessed eyes,
        so blessed are they in their strife.

Yes. Most welcoming in their nature and firm on
faith,
        sipping on coffee, staying up till late.

Yes. Desert at its core, the golden thread through
its body,
        famine disguised with smiles, a true
jihadi.

Yes. The eloquence of their tongues shines
against the dark
        black billowing clouds of ballistic
bombardment.

Yemen: the land of hope and peace as its
adornment.

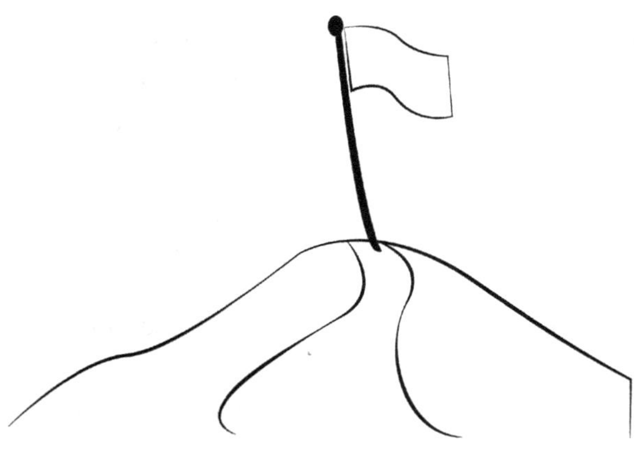

The End of the Narcissist

All his deceit is finally painted into the picture;
You see the red flags dotted in the polluted sea.
Over time, he became your greatest accuser,
So you could crumble and he would relish in the
debris.

Silence. 'I've destroyed your life', he said.

"Friends" all turned away one by one,
Dropping like infected fingers.

'I've destroyed your life', he said.

His enablers and flying monkeys round you up,
Covering people's ears and veiling their eyes.
Society gossips when your back is turned,
And he walks away, smiling at his smear
campaign,
Conjuring up another plan for his next game.

'I've destroyed your life', he said,
And walked away, like a haunting ghost.

Heavenly Realities

My spirit travelled a million seas,
But its yearning was never satisfied.
It has felt your presence in the cool breeze,
And seen the splendour of your holy lights.

A burning thirst sips from cups of knowledge,
And carries my burdens to places true,
Just to be in a blessed assemblage,
So this plant can enjoy the morning dew.

Help me row and overcome the tempests.
Help me drop my anchor; I'm home again.
No return, homeward bound, a wondrous test,
Envelop me with love, always, amen.

On the other side, we'll embrace once more,
Heavenly realities, like before.

The Darkest Alleys of Love

I'm a wandering soul,
On nights so cold,
The darkest alleys of love
I roam.
I can play hide and seek,
When things look bleak,
In the dark alleys of love;
It's home.

I sing a lullaby
To beautify
Their black, solitary sadness,
A dome,
Encapsulating them,
A chronic phlegm,
In the dark alleys of love,
Alone.

Tears run like waterfalls,
At lovers' calls.
In the darkest alleys of love
They groan.
They stupidly lose sleep,
As the guilt creeps,

Paralysing them with fear;
They moan.

Don't believe them when they,
Say it's too late.
Through love's dark, cheating alleys
I've flown.
Tonight, don't you give up,
On all your luck,
The darkest alleys of love
Atone.

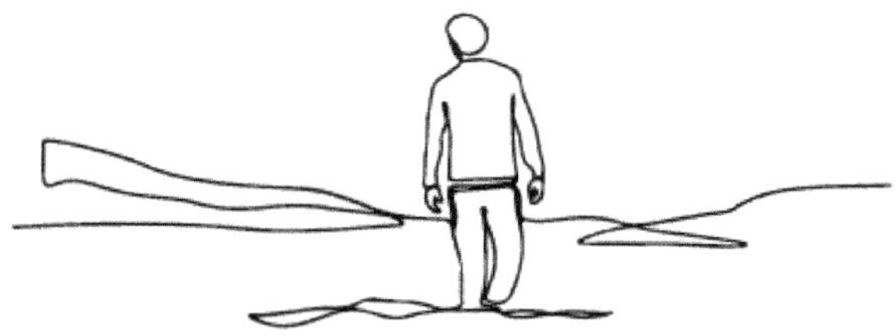

My Saving Grace

I found you on the scorching desert plain,
Where life stood still and darkness surrounded.
You provided shelter from the rain,
And all the travails you expounded.

As a crisp, cool leaf in the autumn wind,
I could've been crushed by any creature.
This beautiful disaster was destined,
From a jokester, you became my teacher.

Your sense of humour made me laugh once
more,
Reminding me of the meaning of life,
And that a fire called love burns through my
core
And can ignore my past thrusting a knife.

You left a footprint no other can match,
Then slowly, triumphantly, you detached.

Hope

I hope my voice soothed
       your fluttering heart rate,
That you felt secure
       with the sound of my steady breaths,
And my lullabies
       wrapped you in their warm embrace.
The thought of my soft palm
       against your chest,
My fingers tracing your skin
       in patterns like lace,
Conjures memories of our speech,
       sensually caressed.

I hope there were moments
       you laughed heartily,
That my wittiness and humour
       set you free from the chains,
And that I wiped clean
       your loneliness casually,
Whilst you appreciated
       my beauty and brains.

I hope you remember
       every fine detail,

Like our first conversation
     and all the common ground.

I still hope our constellations
     don't fail.

That they haven't
     failed.

Overnight Terrorist

Our childhood celebrated multicultural Britain
In the shadows of the tyrannical Gulf War.
We rode on our bikes, carefree, until sundown,
We just weren't prepared for what was in store.

The sound of our laughter echoing in the streets
Was replaced by hushed voices and concealed
hate.
Overnight, we lost our liberty and faith,
Because 9/11 was no longer just a date.

Our childhood taught us to express ourselves,
But the phoney War on Terror slashed off our
tongues.
Secret online searches for injustices were
widespread,
An unknown fear cutting the breath from our
lungs.

The President Saddam Hussain was a masjid,
Not anymore, he was hunted for WMD.
Our communities' fires were extinguished,
Relieved when Mr Begg and the Tipton Three
were set free.

Our childhood consisted of war: Afghanistan,
Iraq.
We witnessed on our screens the horrors of Abu
Ghraib,
And after the largest protest in world history,
We were told by politicians how to behave.

Airport security was nonexistent before
they stood shoulder to shoulder and made us the
other.
The coalition forces became a disease;
Their greed for oil was beginning to smother.

Muhammad Saeed al-Sahhaf's courage
Was worth more than their Baghdad Bob
mockery.
Our childhood won't forget the story of Ali,
When they chopped his limbs, then awarded his
bravery.

We lived in Britain, the land of the "civilised",
But our hearts were with those who they wished
to defeat.
Blowing up media outlets was revolting,
Meanwhile, we were forced to take a backseat.

Terrorism, Islamist, Islamophobia,
These words didn't exist in my vocabulary.

I became an overnight terrorist.
How we rose from this hijacked fall is
extraordinary.

Dragons and Demons

Every now and then, a beast rears its head
In a forest from long ago.
Nestled in a violet flower bed,
It's made melancholy its home.

Protective, like a fire-breathing dragon
Don't get too close or it will kill.
It's living for a timely ascension
To be released from this bastille.

Flashes of its purple underbelly,
The jet black of its scales and skin,
Strong, firm wings will turn your legs to jelly;
Don't wrongly accuse it of sin.

Every now and then, many demons rise,
Claiming its knowledge for their own.
Clueless about this beast's flawless goodbyes
And how its fires destroy to stone.

Rat Race

Did you stop to notice the morning dew,
And the chirping of the birds as the daylight
breaks?
Did you stop to notice the changing of the
seasons,
And the rays of sunshine reflecting off the lake?

Did you stop to notice the colours of the dusk,
And how they blend into each other like
emotions?
Did you stop to notice the roaring thunderstorm,
And the fierce waves of the unforgiving oceans?

Too busy running in this rat race to feel the
breeze,
Preoccupied with climbing up the ladder.
Did you forget how the stars light up the night
skies,
Or will the sight of the full moon make you
madder?

Stop and notice the wonders of the Earth,
The love of the Universe as it seeps into the
world.

A job that will replace you, doesn't know your
worth.
A bank balance is not what should come first.

Did you stop to notice how your muscles ache,
And the groaning of your back as you lie in bed?
You can't ignore the stinging in your eyes when
you wake.
In the end, this rat race won't help you when
you're dead.

A Letter to the Old Me

Dear Old Me,

Wear your scrapes of triumph with pride
And know these tears come with lessons;
Focus on the magic beyond this life,
And view the rife misconduct as oppression.

Remember who you used to be,
That spark of life, that burning passion;
This event is a Divine decree,
Written by the Pen of predestination.

The ink was swirled into the sky,
Sealing your fate with the glittering stars.
You don't need anyone to help you fly,
When it is God Himself who treats these scars.

Forgive yourself and get up off the floor,
Put this dissociation to a stop.
Escape from depression's corridor;
Understand there's no flight without a drop.

Conditions improve, if only you knew,
There's a role designed for you to play.
Your eyes will notice a different hue,

Taking most of the old shadows away.

Yours truly,

New You

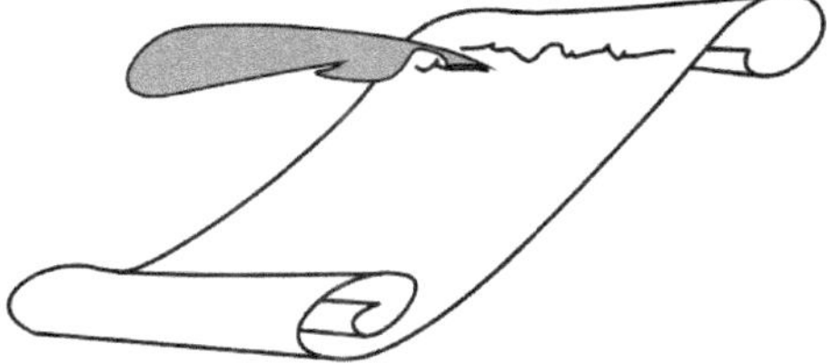

Cycle of Guidance

I never thought I'd stumble upon
Such purity and faith magnified.
Your colour's green and you radiate love,
Watching me from somewhere up above:

Your status reaches the mighty Heavens,
And your guidance revives my poor soul.
Slowly but surely, a step at a time,
I learn to put my heart over mind.

You show me an alternative way;
It's new terrain but I'm stumbling on.
The glory of this world is fading,
Replaced by Divine blessings, cascading.

Emanating from your face is a light,
Renewing belief one day at a time.
This Love is comparable to none;
Every day it steers me back to the One.

A collection of poems that can be picked up on any day. Relatable, thought-provoking and bursting with colour, Rainbows and Rainy Days is an anthology for those who have rode the waves of life's struggles and appreciate beauty in the little things.

ABOUT THE AUTHOR

Q. M. Saiyed teaches English Language and Literature in Birmingham, United Kingdom and writes a range of fiction, both poetry and prose, through which wider issues of society and the world are highlighted. Q. M. Saiyed's poetry has previously been published in anthologies by Capsule Stories and Forward Press. In 2020, she landed first place in a fantasy short story competition, which reignited her love and passion for writing. Q. M. Saiyed is currently embarking on the journey of writing her very first novel, with a vision to continue putting pen to paper for years to come.

Instagram handle: q_m_saiyed_writes

9 789357 446822